EASIEST 5-FIN
PIANO COLLEC

Elton John

15 classic Elton John songs
arranged for 5-finger piano

Information on free material
downloadable to your computer
32

Wise Publications
part of The Music Sales Group
London / New York / Paris / Sydney / Copenhagen / Berlin / Madrid / Tokyo

ROCKET MAN

Words & Music by Elton John & Bernie Taupin

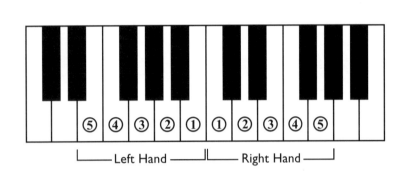

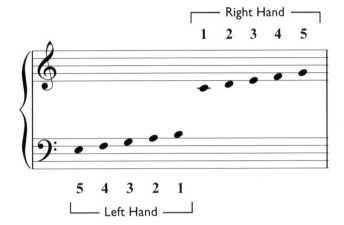

Steadily ♩ = 138

And I think it's gon - na be a long,___ long

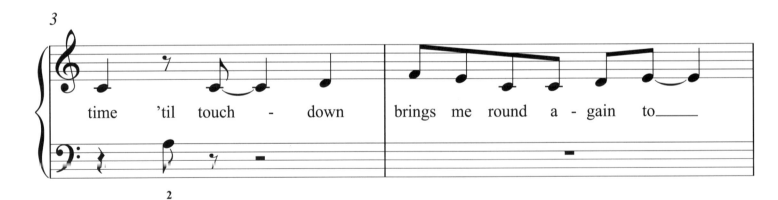

time 'til touch - down brings me round a - gain to___

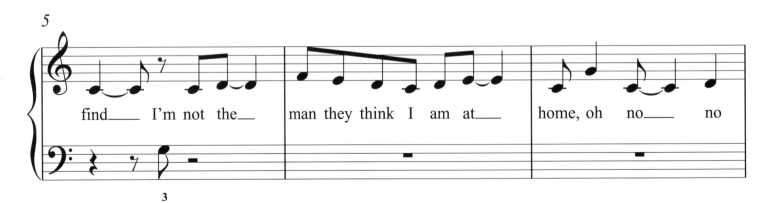

find___ I'm not the___ man they think I am at___ home, oh no___ no

BLUE EYES

Words & Music by Elton John & Gary Osborne

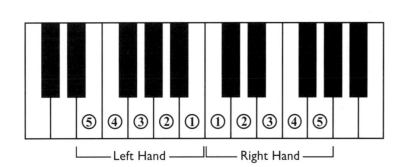

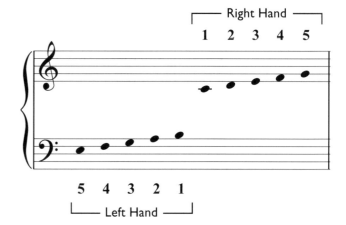

Lazy swing ♩ = 72

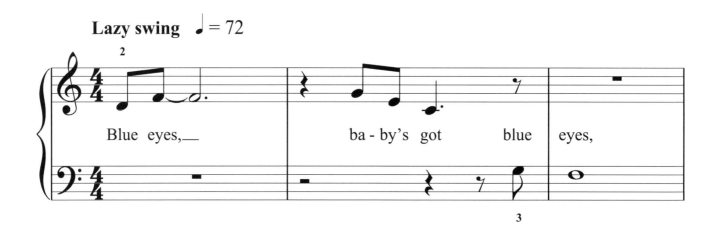

Blue eyes,— ba-by's got blue eyes,

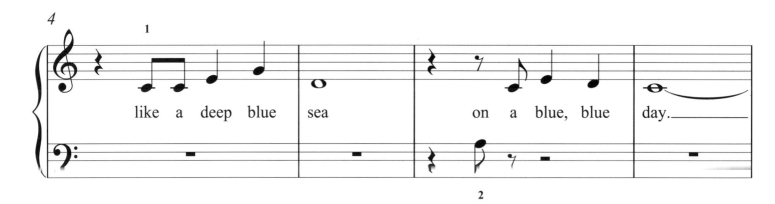

like a deep blue sea on a blue, blue day.

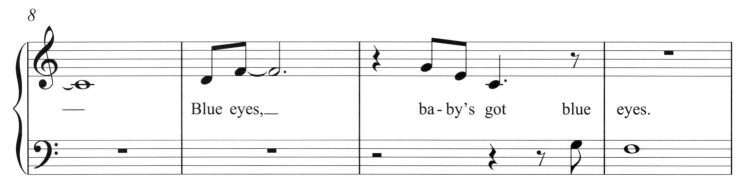

— Blue eyes,— ba-by's got blue eyes.

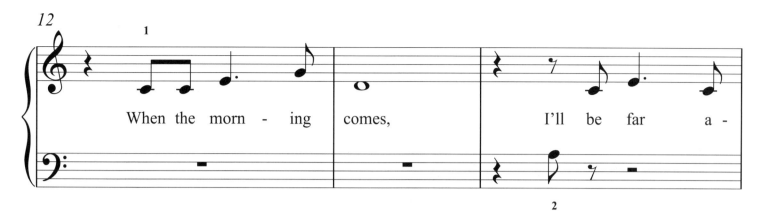

When the morn - ing comes, I'll be far a -

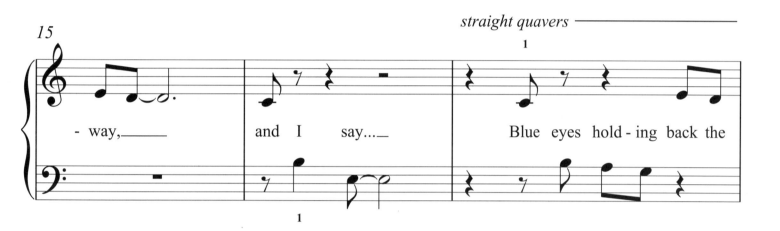

straight quavers

- way,_____ and I say..._ Blue eyes hold - ing back the

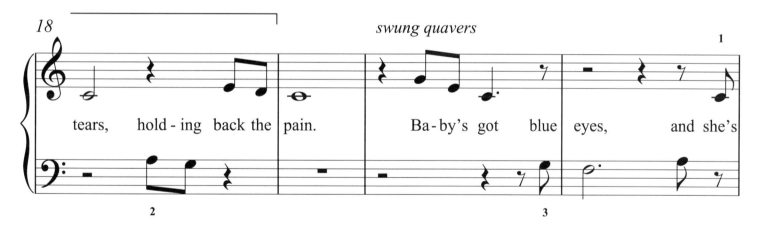

swung quavers

tears, hold - ing back the pain. Ba - by's got blue eyes, and she's

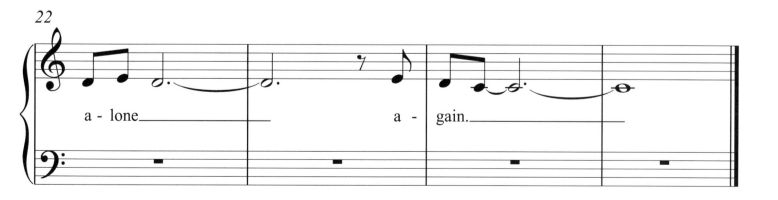

a - lone_____ a - gain.____

CANDLE IN THE WIND

Words & Music by Elton John & Bernie Taupin

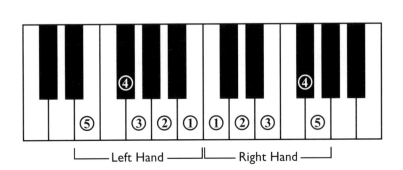
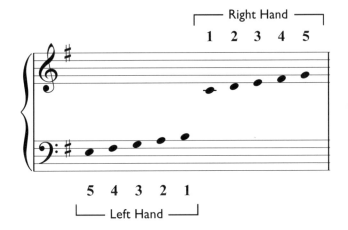

Tenderly ♩ = 120

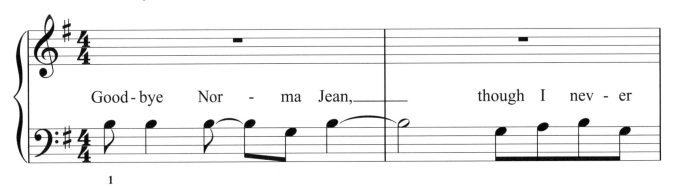

Good - bye   Nor - ma Jean,_____   though I nev - er

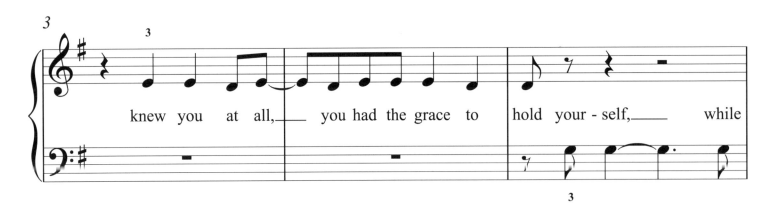

knew you   at all,____   you had the grace to   hold your - self,____   while

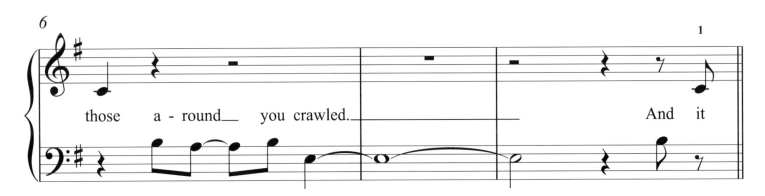

those   a - round__ you crawled._____   And it

YOUR SONG

Words & Music by Elton John & Bernie Taupin

© Copyright 1969 Dick James Music Limited.
Universal/Dick James Music Limited.
All rights in Germany administered by Universal Music Publ. GmbH.
All Rights Reserved. International Copyright Secured.

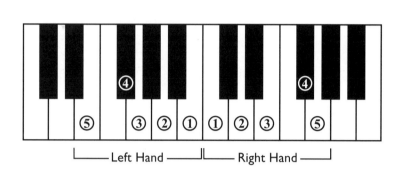

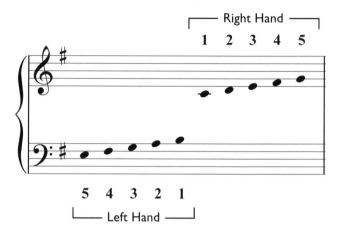

Tenderly ♩ = 120

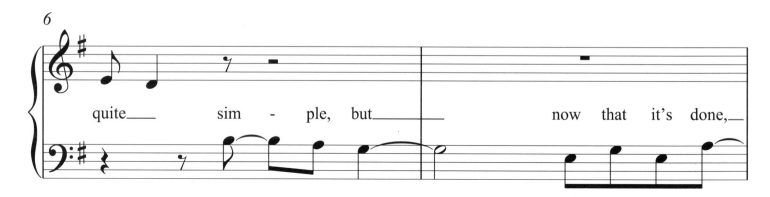

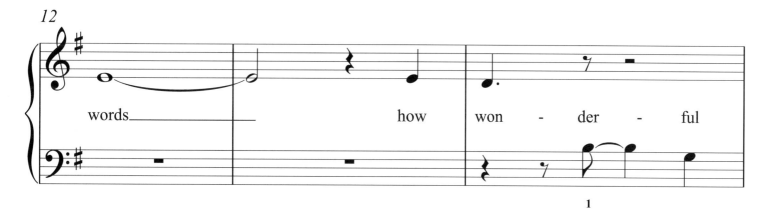

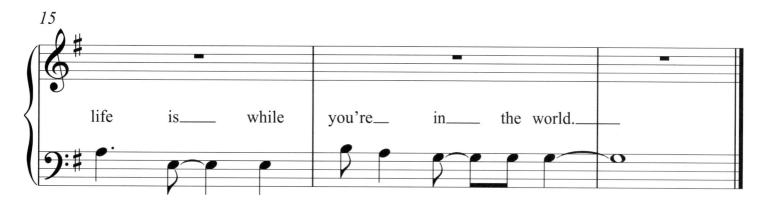

CROCODILE ROCK

Words & Music by Elton John & Bernie Taupin

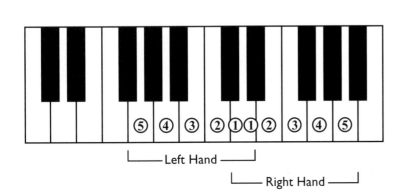

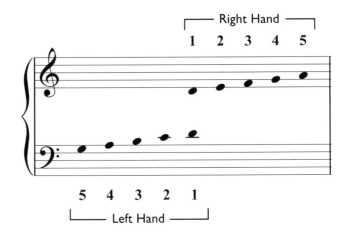

Upbeat Rock 'n' Roll ♩ = 138

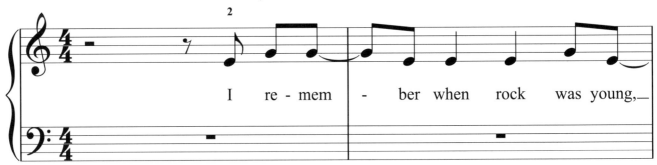

I re-mem - ber when rock was young,

me and Su - zie had so much fun, holding hands

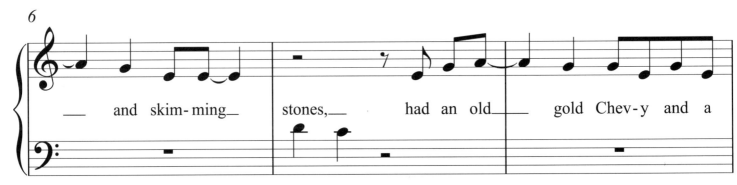

and skim-ming stones, had an old gold Chev-y and a

DANIEL

Words & Music by Elton John & Bernie Taupin

© Copyright 1972 Dick James Music Limited.
Universal/Dick James Music Limited.
All rights in Germany administered by Universal Music Publ. GmbH.
All Rights Reserved. International Copyright Secured.

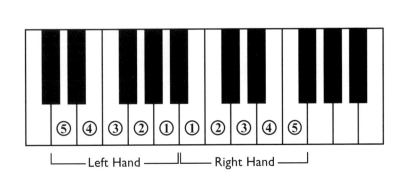

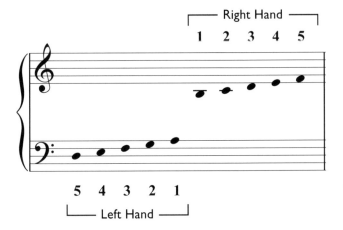

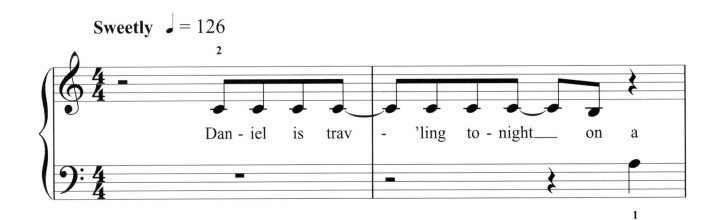

Dan - iel is trav - 'ling to - night___ on a

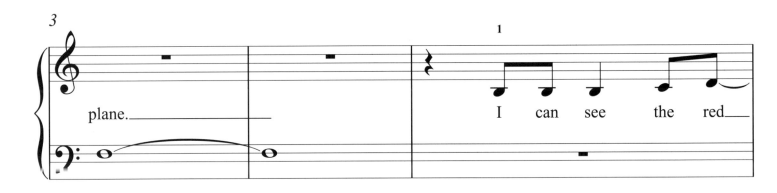

plane.___ I can see the red

___ tail - lights___ head - ing to Spain,___ oh,___ and___

SHINE ON THROUGH

Words & Music by Elton John & Gary Osborne

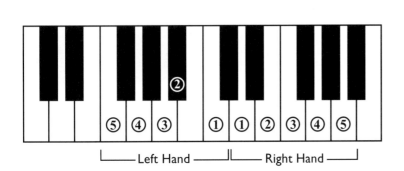

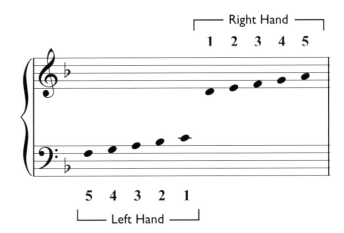

Expressively ♩ = 92

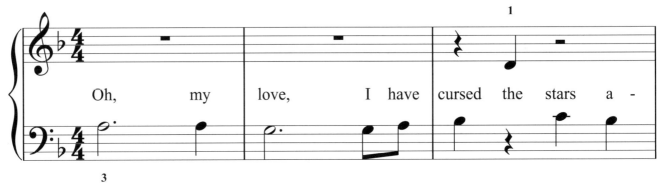

Oh, my love, I have cursed the stars a-

-bove that led my heart to

you. But as hard as I

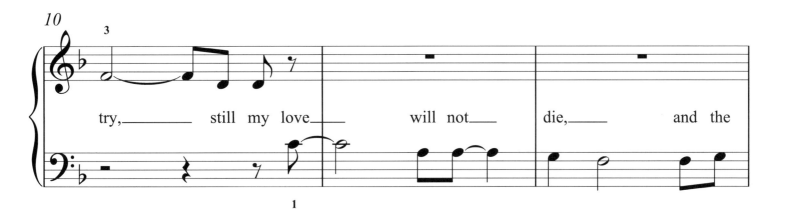

try,_____ still my love_____ will not_____ die,_____ and the

stars_____ still shine on through._____

And the stars_____ still

shine on through._____

SOMEONE SAVED MY LIFE TONIGHT

Words & Music by Elton John & Bernie Taupin

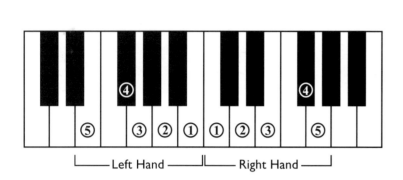

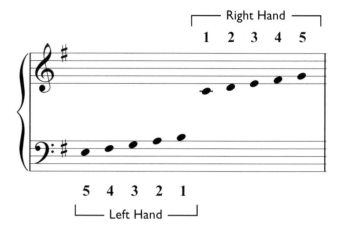

With feeling ♩ = 66

Some - one saved my life to - night,____

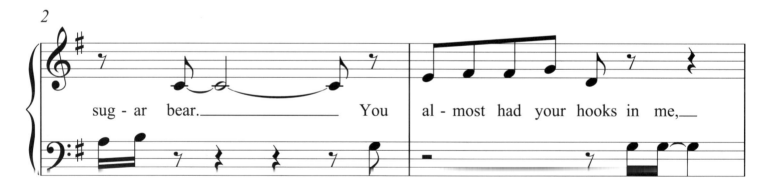

sug - ar bear.____ You al - most had your hooks in me,____

didn't you dear?____ You near - ly had me roped____ and tied,

al-tar-bound,_ hyp-no-tized;_ sweet free-dom whis-pered in my ear, 'you're a

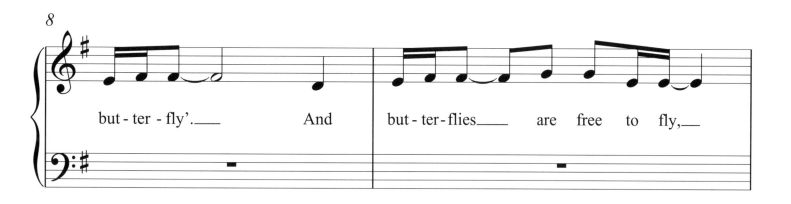

but-ter-fly'._ And but-ter-flies__ are free to fly,__

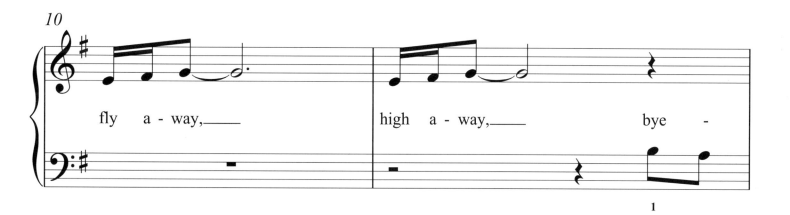

fly a - way,___ high a - way,___ bye -

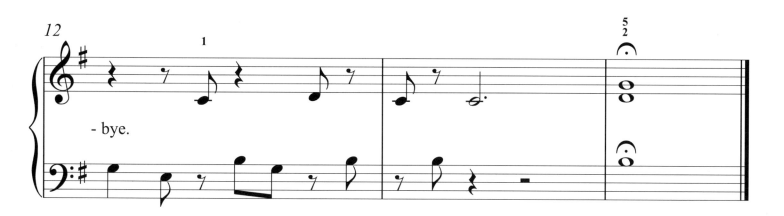

- bye.

I GUESS THAT'S WHY THEY CALL IT THE BLUES

Words & Music by Elton John, Bernie Taupin & Davey Johnstone
© Copyright 1983 HST Management Limited/Rouge Booze Incorporated/Big Pig Music Limited.
Universal Music Publishing Limited.
All rights in Germany administered by Universal Music Publ. GmbH.
All Rights Reserved. International Copyright Secured.

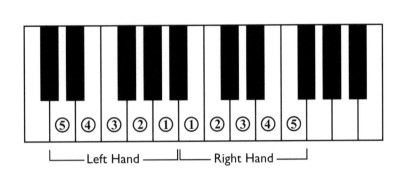

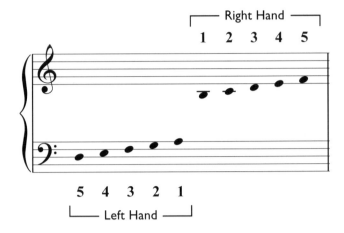

Lazily swung ♩ = 80

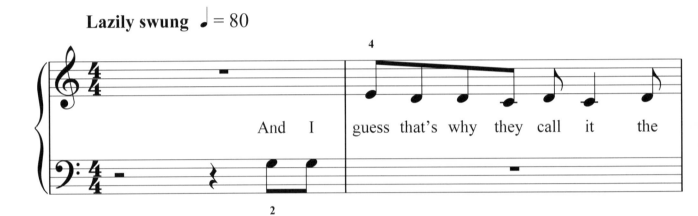

And I guess that's why they call it the

blues. Time on my hands could be time spent with

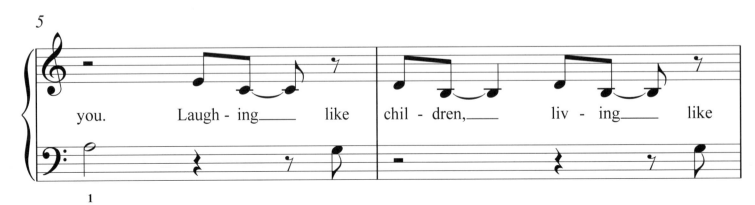

you. Laugh - ing like chil - dren, liv - ing like

BELIEVE

Words & Music by Elton John & Bernie Taupin

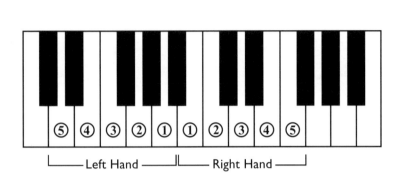

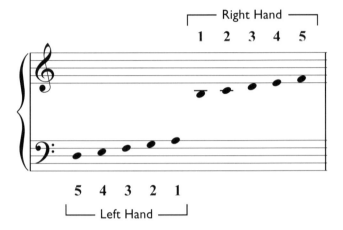

Confidently ♩ = 69

I be-lieve in love, it's all we got.

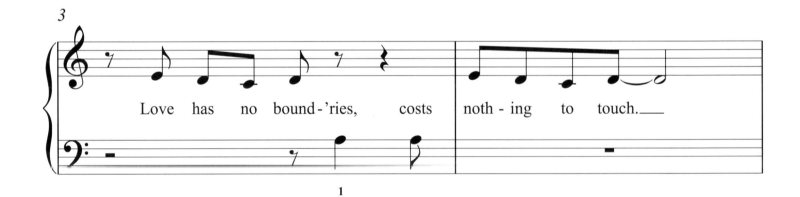

Love has no bound-'ries, costs noth-ing to touch.

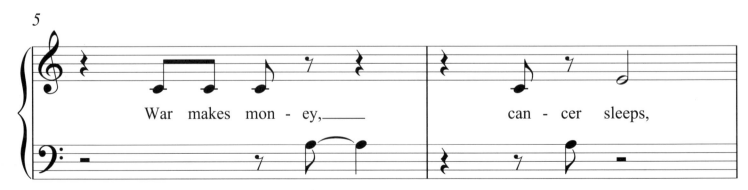

War makes mon-ey, can-cer sleeps,

BORDER SONG

Words & Music by Elton John & Bernie Taupin

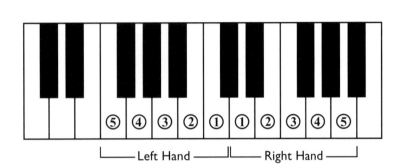

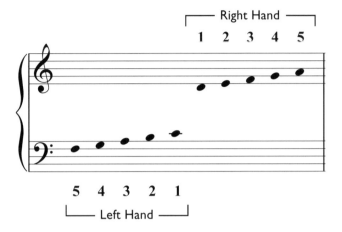

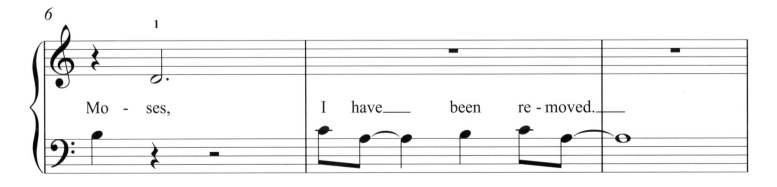

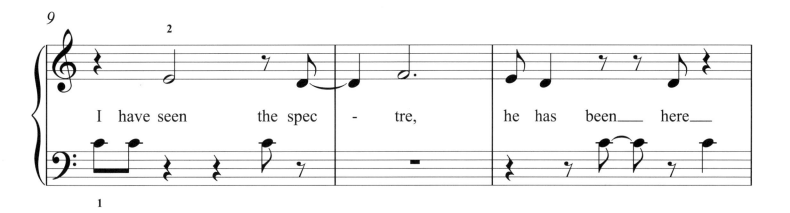

I have seen the spec - tre, he has been here too.

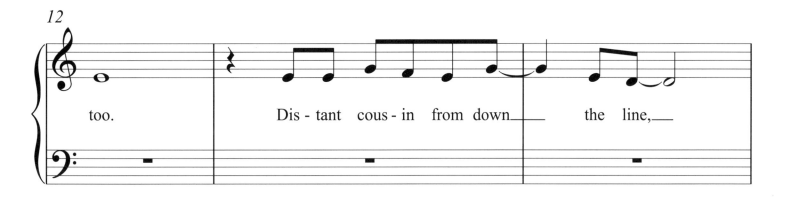

Dis - tant cous - in from down the line,

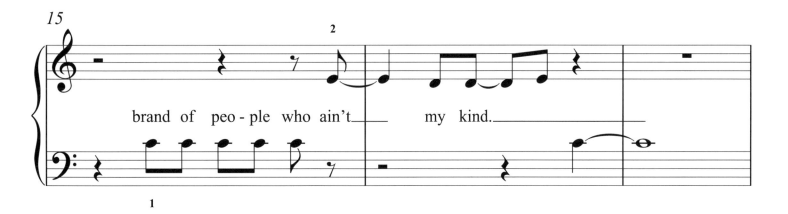

brand of peo - ple who ain't my kind.

Ho - ly Mo - ses, I have been re - moved.

SACRIFICE

Words & Music by Elton John & Bernie Taupin

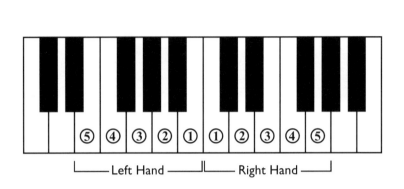

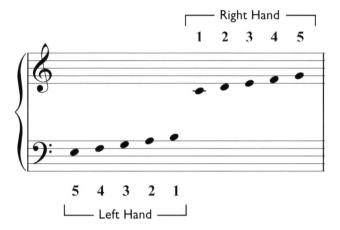

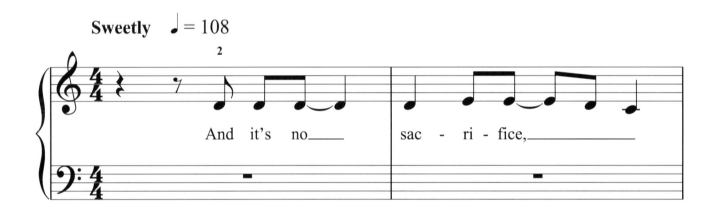

And it's no sac - ri - fice,

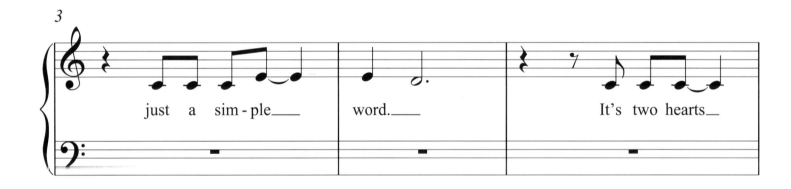

just a sim - ple word. It's two hearts

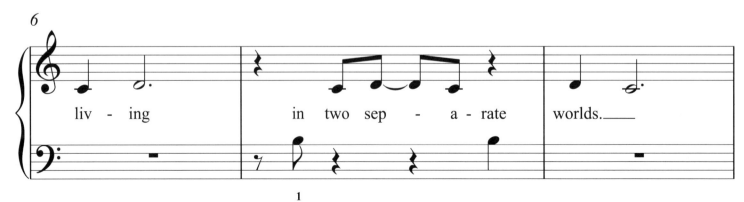

liv - ing in two sep - a - rate worlds.

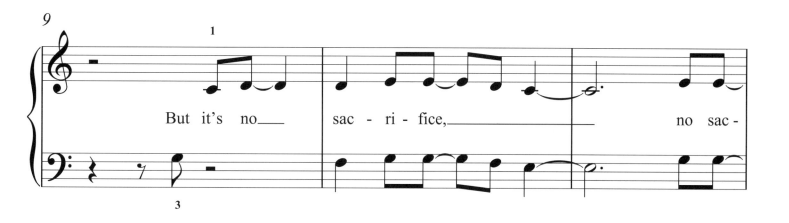

But it's no___ sac - ri - fice,_____ no sac -

- ri - fice,_____ it's no sac - ri - fice_____

__ at_____ all.

No sac - ri - fice_____ at all.

I'M STILL STANDING

Words & Music by Elton John & Bernie Taupin

© Copyright 1983 HST Management Limited/Rouge Booze Incorporated.
Universal Music Publishing Limited.
All rights in Germany administered by Universal Music Publ. GmbH.
All Rights Reserved. International Copyright Secured.

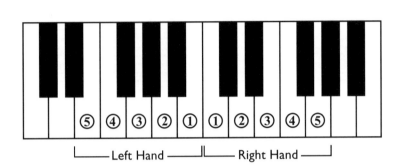

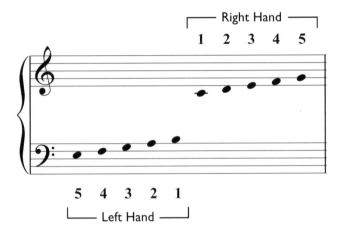

Energetically swung ♩ = 144

Don't you know, I'm still stand - ing bet - ter than I

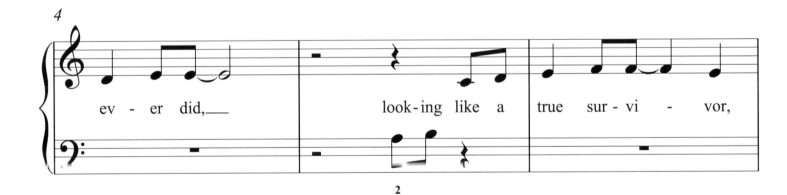

ev - er did,___ look - ing like a true sur - vi - vor,

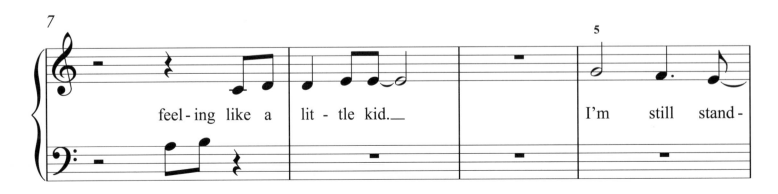

feel - ing like a lit - tle kid.___ I'm still stand -

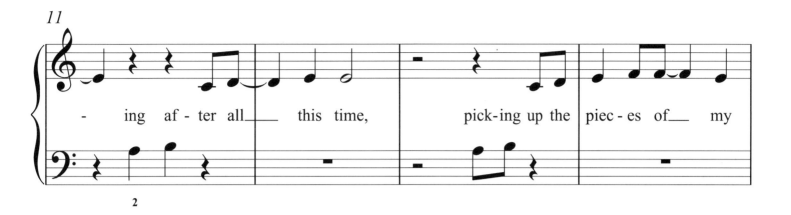

-ing af - ter all___ this time, pick-ing up the piec - es of___ my

life with - out you on my mind.___ I'm___ still stand -ing,

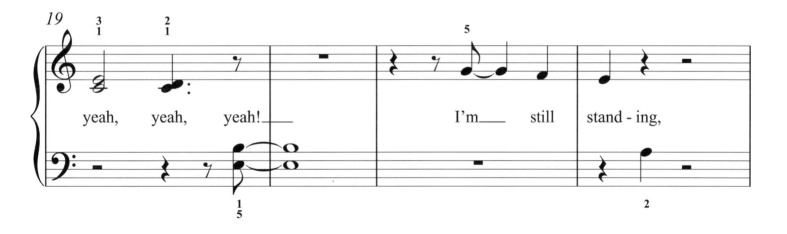

yeah, yeah, yeah!___ I'm___ still stand - ing,

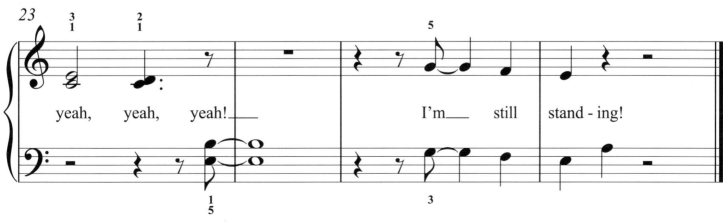

yeah, yeah, yeah!___ I'm___ still stand - ing!

DON'T LET THE SUN GO DOWN ON ME

Words & Music by Elton John & Bernie Taupin

© Copyright 1974 HST Management Limited/Rouge Booze Incorporated.
Universal Music Publishing Limited.
All rights administered in Germany by Universal Music Publ. GmbH.
All Rights Reserved. International Copyright Secured.

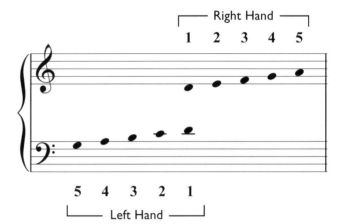

Powerfully ♩ = 69

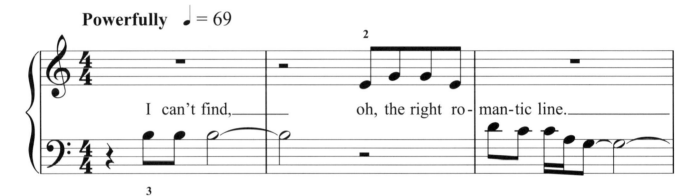

I can't find, oh, the right ro-man-tic line.

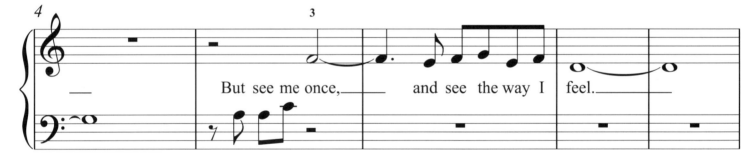

But see me once, and see the way I feel.

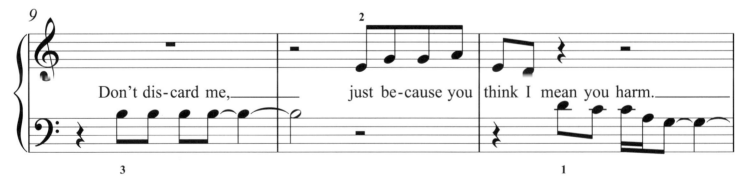

Don't dis-card me, just be-cause you think I mean you harm.

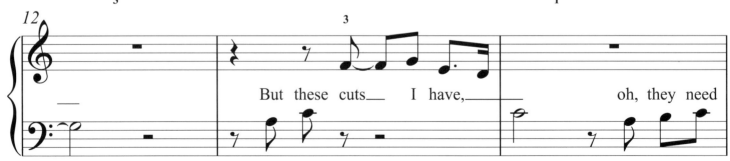

But these cuts I have, oh, they need

DON'T GO BREAKING MY HEART

Words & Music by Ann Orson & Carte Blanche

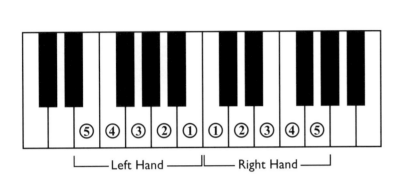

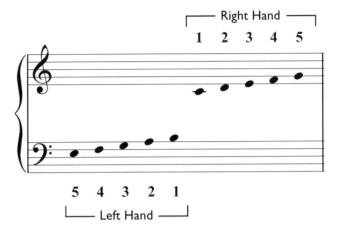

123456789

EASIEST 5-FINGER PIANO COLLECTION
ALSO AVAILABLE IN THE SERIES...

Abba
A great collection of
15 classic Abba hits,
including 'Dancing
Queen', 'Fernando', 'Take
A Chance On Me' and
'Thank You For The Music'.
AM998404

Ballads
A superb collection of
15 well-known ballads,
including 'Fix You',
'I Have A Dream', 'Let
It Be' and 'What A
Wonderful World'.
AM995346

The Beatles
15 classic Beatles hits
including 'All My
Loving', 'Hey Jude',
'She Loves You' and
'Yellow Submarine'.
NO91322

Chart Hits
15 popular chart hits
including 'About You
Now', 'Bleeding Love',
'Clocks', 'Foundations',
'Shine' and 'Umbrella'.
AM995357

Classical Favourites
15 classical pieces
including 'Jupiter' (Holst),
'Lullaby ' (Brahms),
'Minuet In G' (J.S. Bach)
and 'Spring' (Vivaldi).
AM998393

Film Songs
15 great film songs
including 'Breaking
Free', 'Don't Worry, Be
Happy', 'Somewhere
Out There' and 'You've
Got A Friend In Me'.
AM995335

Showtunes
15 great showtunes
including 'Any Dream
Will Do', 'Circle Of Life',
'Mamma Mia' and 'My
Favourite Things'.
AM995324

Today's Hits
15 of today's current
chart hits including
'Hallelujah', 'Human',
'If I Were A Boy' and
'Viva La Vida'.
AM998415

Download to your computer a set of piano accompaniments for this *Elton John* edition
(to be played by a teacher/parent).
Visit: **www.hybridpublications.com**
Registration is free and easy.
Your registration code is RJ989

Published by
Wise Publications
14-15 Berners Street,
London W1T 3LJ, UK.

Exclusive Distributors:
Music Sales Limited
Distribution Centre, Newmarket Road,
Bury St Edmunds, Suffolk IP33 3YB, UK.
Music Sales Pty Limited
20 Resolution Drive, Caringbah,
NSW 2229, Australia.

Order No. AM1001099
ISBN 978-1-84938-614-2
This book © Copyright 2010 Wise Publications,
a division of Music Sales Limited.

Edited by Lizzie Moore
Arranging and engraving supplied by Camden Music.

Printed in the EU.

Your Guarantee of Quality
As publishers, we strive to produce every
book to the highest commercial standards.
This book has been carefully designed to
minimise awkward page turns and to
make playing from it a real pleasure.
Particular care has been given to specifying acid-free,
neutral-sized paper made from pulps which have
not been elemental chlorine bleached.
This pulp is from farmed sustainable forests and was
produced with special regard for the environment.
Throughout, the printing and binding have been
planned to ensure a sturdy, attractive publication
which should give years of enjoyment.
If your copy fails to meet our high standards,
please inform us and we will gladly replace it.

www.musicsales.com